TRACERY

ALSO BY EDWARD BYRNE

Aporia

Beautiful Lies

*Duets**

A Flea the Size of Paris: The Old French fatrasies *&* fatras
(with Donato Mancini)

*The Recovery of the Public World: Essays on Poetics in
Honour of Robin Blaser* (co-edited with Charles Watts)*

Sonnets : Louise Labé

* Published by Talonbooks

TRACERY

POEMS

EDWARD BYRNE

TALONBOOKS

Talonbooks
9259 Shaughnessy Street, Vancouver, British Columbia, Canada v6p 6r4
talonbooks.com

Talonbooks is located on xʷməθkʷəẏəm, Sḵwx̱wú7mesh, and səl̓ilwətaɁɬ
Lands.

First printing: 2022

Typeset in Arno
Printed and bound in Canada on 100% post-consumer recycled paper

Cover illustration and design by Ginger Sedlarova
Interior design by Typesmith

Talonbooks acknowledges the financial support of the Canada Council
for the Arts, the Government of Canada through the Canada Book Fund,
and the Province of British Columbia through the British Columbia Arts
Council and the Book Publishing Tax Credit.

Library and Archives Canada Cataloguing in Publication

Title: Tracery : poems / Edward Byrne.
Names: Byrne, Edward, 1947- author.
Identifiers: Canadiana 20220141746 | ISBN 9781772014358 (softcover)
Subjects: LCGFT: Poetry.
Classification: LCC PS8553.Y713 T73 2022 | DDC C811/.54—dc23

for Paul Kelley

(TRACER)

Morning cold
fingers tips
and nose tip
cold and damp
behind ears rims

as a shiver
in a dream
of contention
over magistery

2

(Inter arma silent musae)

In the middle distance
a culture of alarums
of grand schemes
out of hand

this grey noon
capital is empire

fifteen cops
one thief
and a crowd

3

Behind the weather
the storm

behind a
rhetoric of clouds

Behind capital
the war

at odds
with the adages
argument conceals

(TRACE)

1

A habit broken
taken up again

down here the lyric
goes without saying
the news escapes me

Above on the porch
my blue iris
two weeks early
or three years late

2

Rain as in
rainforest
downs my last iris

I expect
a dram of whisky
smooth as flesh

at my age
bedraggled

almonds and raisins

3

Perilous gulf
death opened
cracks a costly shell

Our father
his mouth
a shadow
yawning

no last words
only a rattle
from some depth

4
(jeder immer)

Pantalon
en chino
délavé
authentique
qui assure
la durabilité
et le confort
de votre pantalon
usé préferé

Like an old
pair of pants
back from
the laundry

always
already worn
and just like new
it will last
forever

5

A murder
of crows
before dawn
mocks choristry
from low branches

pissed off they
strut armlessly
across the lawn
lacking all grace

6

Eyes burn
after climbing
page by page
the declension
of hills by water

Imbricated
a white dahlia
a red wine
that tempers heresy

(TRAC)

1

Music invisible
disappears
so strange
it's written
that music
appears and
is not heard
reappears
without a word

2

Lust creates
a vacuum
an eternity
of pleasures
just as though
nothing happened here

Perhaps it's because
I come from the provinces
where there are no certainties

3

In an age of carts
intercourse
is simply a measure
of like and unlike

In an era of calculation
commerce
is entirely based
on the equivalence
of like and dislike

(TRA)

1

(Pox Americana)

We attend
a long and anxious moment
of undisturbed calm
in our cave of carpets and books
that mute the signals
as if the stench of the dead
had never crossed
the imaginary boundary
of this new century

2

Such a quantity
of spent time
between the lines

If the words
that pass between us
were counted
they would still be few

Mine full of desire
yours perhaps not

3

Adjectives
are insufficient

Verbs are
too precise

Untoward together
insubstantial
they make trial
of the heaped objects
time leaves behind

4

This mechanic music
holds the elements
of its perfection
in homeostatic play

The ideologic of its time
removes me to dumb reflection

Considering
the relation
of lust to proximity

5

The rain comes
from another country
it's so hard
and sudden

like longing
or laughter

Someone says
It's hail
Come look

6

Across an open field
she saw him
coming back to her

Lacy and woven
garbled and lyric
these notes
never taken for signs

She saw him in monk's garb
coming back to her

(TRAM)

1

This day then
like all others
shot through
with the heat
of sidelong glances

And the coincidence
of hail and sunshine
lines of force
takes a moment

2

The ghosts of desire
straddle time

Which is more fearsome
their allure
or their stratagems

Clouds of rhetoric
behind which
my anxiety
and the storms of war

3

Words are things
in poetry and psychosis

Their object's
occluded

Never mind
there are others

Also blocked
and easily found

(TRAME)

1

This morning on Union Street
I saw Arthur Rimbaud on a girl's bicycle

And then
                close behind him
                                Jean Seberg

They smiled at me and waved

Then came Antonin Artaud
weaving and shouting curses

None of them wore helmets

I worry about their heads
which I adore

2

In Strathcona I wondered
in this neighbourhood
if they came to evict
would the neighbours
turn away
or would they
mob the evictors
like the Egyptian workers
I read about this morning

3

This old house on the corner
of McLean and East Pender
where I remember
a kitchen full of poets
and talking about
Tiananmen Square in the garden

is where my irises once grew
still tumbledown
derelict from all eternity

4

She adjusts the back of her pants
to display her tattoo
before hoisting herself
onto the roof of the BMW

A blonde in a Mustang convertible
crosses the path of my memories

I pause at the Jimi Hendrix shrine
stop at the Wicklow Pub to salute
the Cartesian Centaur

5

Little houses behind high hedges
secret gardens and green utopian moments
but no squats and no campers in the park

Young girls on bikes catch my eye
You oughta wear a helmet I think

A shirtless old man
with a big red wig and painted face
shouts It's beautifuller to be a girl

You got that right one of them shouts back

6

If wishing could make it so
he'd still be there on his porch
a Stoic leafing through pages
but he never is

And I never see Louis
as I imagine him
on the Union Market patio
an Epicurean eating ice cream
listening to the loud birds

(TRAMER)

1

On the borderline
of day
light disturbs
the illuminations
of insistent sadness

A comedy half over
promises much laughter
says the old man
turning over
to hold off the dawn

2

And laughter's
only the half of it

Begin again
Mehitabel
nouveau-née
with firm feet
and stanzas
full of
broken furniture

3
(The Funnies)

I wanted to say
more than nine lines aloud
I meant to say
more than nine lives allowed
no not that and not the other

Verdichtung = condensation
a lessening and a getting
slowly to that one line
that brickbat Ignatz lobs

MORNING SONGS

1

Making
or finding
a knowing
a morning
like this
a broken word
reassembled

2

If the wind
is a god
then morning
is an afterthought
its breath
on my face
a gift
from the corridor
of leaves

3

Abandoned
a blessing
sought
after time

The city
questions
the wind's
disordered ways

4

Left here
to my devices
I stagger
my hours
brief service
the politics
of lost powers

5

That which holds us
in the long line
of day's refusal
drops from the horizon
dawn's emerald
not a ring
not a bond
an arrival

6

You are a point of no return
this and every morning
where my thoughts
exit from dream's grasp
never grasped
all the little signs
all your stars blinking out

7

Syncopated
rhythms of morning
divide my attention
between you and you
a seeking after
and a taking in
hidden
behind that cloud

8

Morning after morning
the residue of dreams
inches toward noon

The light dwindles
in proportion
to the distance
it travels

9

After noon a wind
caressed my thoughts
remembering a bank
of morning glories
by the bog

Love will be lysergic
or not at all

10

Morning morning
green and rose
banks of peat moss
the supernal
drawn down here
Labrador tea

11

I saw Kirilov
fifty years ago
on the Barton Street bus
and again this morning
on 6th Avenue

One of us hasn't changed
in all those years

12

This morning
after the first
of three storms
I wept
in a dream
of home
incessant patter
of rain on the deck

13

Surprised
by the moan
of the bank door
as I passed through
an animate sadness
a mourning played by ear

14

In this snap
my heart joins
a chorus of sparrows
in a beech tree
on Union Street
confronted
with the ease of song

15

Call it wedding dress
or call it shroud
the morning
delights in subterfuge

After resting
from the weight
of our body
a sheet a comma
a bowl of coffee

16

Morning raises
melancholic prayer
a sense of loss
across an addled sensorium

Bring me Bavarian gentians
Bring me Je Reviens
wafted close tempered
high notes of flute stops
Saint Julien and a Chaliapin
mottled soft skin

17

Morning over lake
of forgotten dreams
claws without copula
or object
remembering her from parts
the ironing board
the garments
the coffee pot
the cup

18

In the silence predicted
by an anthropology
of crowns and wings
of tails and claws
the task encumbered dawn
drew me back to Augustine

The fear of salvation
housed in the architecture
of crumbling backroad courts

19

Café society
a forest of voices
and song
as if morning
were eternal
and writing
suspended
in a claustral embrace
for a thousand years

20

Quickly quickly
dawn spreads
sealing ordinary needs
and you
distant as skin
lie between
sorrow and melancholy
love and ashes

21

Woke this morning
without the burden
of love and loss

Cold air of October
ate my hopes
as I returned
to where I fell

The crows
at war
in the high branches

22

Not morning
it's Antonin Artaud
on the bus

Red scarf
tight black pants
railing and gesturing

Toothless grin
I adore

23

Back across
a bridge of sighs
mud-splattered seascape
leaving behind
an enchanted forest
of hats and scarves and boots
a world made liveable
by design
a dream of dresses

24

Morning
in night's debt
a hare's breath
from the pivot point
of generation

Simply to laud
with silence
the shattered
remnants of law

25

In a pastiche
of morning
the clown
repositions the sacred
there where reliance
on light
bears darkness
in its fold

26

When does the time before us
become the time that remains

Crossing the bridge of sighs
I'll wait for you on the other side

True love I have found you
because an ox took me my dear
I still chase the north wind
mistaking it for a thief

(Watriquet & Raimmondin)

27

A lost continent
of content lost
never to be found
passed on the stair
the before of him
adored in its noon
the now of babble
the sweet trust
of incontinence
and wobble

28

Enjoinment
which is to say
not a word
but the befuddlement
of two languages

Two words for up
two words for down
two ways of saying gone
and two ways of saying here

29

Knowing not grasping time
not measure but vision
finding its internal push
making visible dehiscent beauty

Morning rain that drenched
the yard the sun the night
and us down by Pompey
entangled in the garden shed
in the forgetting of time

30

Morning become morn
the scene of dreaming
lost in diminishing dark
a sparkling tableau
firing between words
a done thing or a doing
beginning a long going
or just plain darkling

TRANSLATION

1

Finally an hour to rejoice in
past winter past song
aided by sleep's idle talk
and these idle thoughts
lodged in cramped hand
working that translation   (Blaser)
past the point of return

2

The wayward conveyance
of these small songs
against the fog of morning
before the rain
by sleight of hand
where the letters are mobile
a variant tuning
by the ear's fine judgment

3
(Cello Suite No. 3)

Arid joy a slowness of assent
brought to heights notwithstanding
as if poetry were a dance of the mind

A clutter of anticipation   a gift
not solace but exercises
as if words were finally enough

Waiting for yet another spring
on doit trafiquer quelque chose
en attendant le jour qui vient   (Aragon)

4

A wind arose
behind the rain
and lent delight
to a hampered walk

The dark sheltered us
from the plague
soaking thought with light

5

What he meant was
wisdom closes thought

Rather what Helen sought
by not being in Troy

translated to Egypt
seeking transference
beyond the capture
of heroes and gods

6

Brunetto's fault
was not sodomy

(pedagogus ergo sodomiticus
as was commonly said)

but the lesson
that we make our own eternity
come l'uom s'etterna   (Dante)
making a world to live in

7

A scattering of honey
where the voice may lie
sweetened by the breath of another

Lines of trembling thought
brought back from the juncture
of comedy and error

Our tongue renders
what the ear hears
in its dwindling eternity

8

Choosing from a lexicon
of words half seen
in their lucidity

striking a match
to briefly light the way
across a boundary
of our own devising
across a bridge of sighs

9

Evening lamp my companion
you still can't light the soul
(we might get lost there)
but the declivity is lit

The study lamp wishes
the reader would pause
and look its way
eyes lifted from the book

(Your simplicity suppresses an angel)

(Rilke)

10

(Après coup)

On the breath of arrows
springtide discloses
a mode of signifying
untethered from its pole

What pleasure there is
in chaining words
one following another
before and after
toward the punctum

11

How much does what we refuse
the Invisible   rule us when
life cedes to the invisible ruse
and becomes invisible again

Slowly by dint of attraction
our centre's displaced
and the heart takes its turn
Grand Master of absence

(Rilke)

12

(Reading *Through the Looking-Glass*)

Nonsense is the backside
of reason's certainty
the fugitive path
from love's grasp

There is danger in clarity
a trespass on ordinary pleasure
at the point beyond
the mirror's reach

13

Sometimes the moon
slips by in the dark
a thin cup of borrowed light
appears and disappears
capricious and true

The night seems to celebrate
approximate time
in the remnants of rain

14

(Eaux d'artifice)

An endless descent reaching up
and tumbling back on yourself
encumbered by earth oh fountain
column of a self-destructive temple

Each jet dancing in transfigured time
silent delirium of night
held in each watery breath

(Rilke, Anger, Deren)

15

Breath informs measure
as it punctuates life
tracing a course through leaves
like a breeze of letters

Counting borrowed time
in discordant intervals
arriving somehow there
where the breath is bated

16

Waiting for evening
waiting for dawn
the earth turning
toward tomorrow

No madness
where a body
of work extends
the time that remains

17

(Window)

Our geometry
simple form effortlessly
circumscribing life

In your frame
what we love expands
into the eternity you offer

All chance abolished
Being captured by love
within this space we master

(Rilke)

18

(Reading *Hermetic Definition*)

Tea of mint or chamomile
for waking or sleeping
with no end in view

Tea obliterates time
as do her eidolons
red roses and *nenuphar*

Late life-cluttered love
the last desperate non-escape (H.D.)

19
(*Ivry*)

those who
demand of me
one brilliant idea
a day
to silence themselves
will roast in
the flames
of Gehenna
forever

(Artaud)

20

The jouissance of an hour
at dawn's late arrival
waking to a conference of birds
and falling back into sleep
where dreams are still welcomed
as thoughts that stave off desire
and the writing on the wall
is translated back across time

DÉLIRES

Je versefie en dormant *

  —Les fatrasies d'Arras

This is what I told them at the Millennium Garage.

Your love, like poetry, requires so much general pleading.

Ho fatto un suono profondo e bello.

Who among us could tell, in this twentieth century, less than the full silence of kings?

Four boys, the voices of Ulysses.

The editor, resigned, trudged to the library in the rain.

Juicy odours in the mind: veronica, jasmine, guerrière.

Can I put butter on my bread?

Taken by the tip of my sorrows and led on the breeze to relent.

I am neither armed nor harmless.

"Can we bore a hole through it?" was one of my father's favourite expressions.

The owl came over and the trees perhaps bled.

These our bodies might not lift against a night of song.

Blasted pine box.

Consistency opens its lid and consents to shame us with its doll-like reveries.

---

* I write these lines in my sleep

Nothing in this world is hopeful except nothing and hope.

We found a lily in the West End, a package from the pope.

A smile is, of a night, summer's tranquil host.

Anything black and edible is called bitumen.

Even successful snowmen must melt.

Struck by a twinge of adolescence.

Pearls and dust.

The last two shots fired in a war are inevitably fired by two tourists leaving the scene of battle.

If we were there in 1971, what would we have seen?

Oh, a regular breakfast with moon cakes.

We must train the dogs in the essence of imaginative surveillance.

I overtook a group of angels. They said that I lacked remorse.

The imagination never stops working, nor do the bandits of time.

Maintenant ils saluent les morts.

What a season for watercolours!

Weight of the century: stupor mundi.

What is Diane doing on the salt wave?

Enough of that, I cannot wear a sweater with a regular hip belt and a thing called meagreness.

There is a point at which the pot cracks.

Nobody was able to show, in any way, at any time, that we were critical of the budget.

Imagine your defeat in a moment of hilarity.

Tell her to send me a hood, if there's nothing else to be learned from excuses.

For all the good that this will do: the form in which the brother achieves exile.

Imagine being without mirrors.

The motorcycle club was like an ocean on the edge of a spoon.

If you have something to hide, hide it among objects of the same kind.

Not in Wickstead, but in Wickham Court.

After hours and hours of preparation, Alice collapsed, having lost the magic knowledge of beginnings.

Are the innocent less certain of their wares?

Prepare your attack – remember the next thing in the mind's eye is a robust cave.

The eternal bird gets the worm.

Eighty miles south of where I live, there's a town called Stasis. That's where I wrote this song.

Freud thus represented several magnitudes of deception.

In Kyoto they say, "Whoever is afraid of politics is also afraid of sin."

An intelligent question is better than a good answer.

His syntax leads him away from telos and into a microcosm of detail.

There are blessed moments that persist only in memory and will lose all substance once we pass the gate.

The problematic moment in any landscape is always the horizon.

In the army his responsibility was to load other people's guns.

The long causeway between pennies.

That's exactly how it is, making a fist out of ostentation.

The very first and the very last rules are always the same.

The smell of devil grass.

Don't just assert, demonstrate.

Sanity, emetically, doesn't offer that many options.

I now have a four-edged sword.

Help me get my missive cleared.

You don't have to think about what it's called to know what it is.

He ceased offering paradoxes and began to offer punts.

Riming is nothing but the conclusion of a thought.

Il n'y a, monsieur, qu'une mare en puces.

I think I'd rather stay and tumble with the divine.

Not through genuflection, but through genuine reflection.

"His safe water," she said, "that drove one dead, was Todesfahr, one that might be deep enough …"

After you return the book, we can have a civilized conversation.

Can there be a rhetoric after Zukofsky?

One couple told me that they had filed seven times for a divorce but were denied every time on the basis of a technicality.

Life is bounded on all sides by infinity.

I came through the motion of my hand in time.

And in the way of intervention stands the massive Book of Justice.

I consulted Einstein and found that everything begins again as soon as the second star reappears.

You see the meeting of pushed grape velvet.

Didn't Bradley say somewhere that Shakespeare was inevitable?

The new century provides a toilet with no flushing sound.

If landed, the derision would be so great it would make the world shake.

My sin is the talk of Istanbul.

Finite sentence type.

My favourite mode of ascent is the ladder.

No silversmith, goldsmith, or mother ever made a finer household effigy.

After all, by the same logic, A = A.

I've decided to write both sides of our correspondence.

There have always been computers.

Where the arrow of time hits the horizon.

Some virtues have no posterity.

Issa, in a fit of passion, invoked a child in a redingote.

I return the sentence to its sheath.

The continuous structure of this sequence suggests that these are not actually dreams.

Those days are rare when you can lucubrate content for the pure joy of it.

Our hearts are stored in our heads.

Temptation would not exist if we did not have inordinate desires.

Jelly for the private parts, not jam.

Do not harm me, says the Mother of the Children of God.

It's a gift, being able to factor in reality.

You are as close as you can get to Forestat's hate from the balcony of a church.

This boy touches the purple crust of heaven, a page from Ganymede's notebook.

History is impossible to write from the inside.

By being allusive I have floated to the surface of time.

A NOTE ON ˙TRANSLATION˙

"Translation" is a coda to the two sections that precede it. It is meant to address those sections somewhat in the manner of the congedo (tornado, envoi) of an Italian canzone. It's not offered as explanation (flattening out), but rather as an excursus or reflection on method, on practice – a poetics. Translation, as a very broadly understood practice, shifts the burden of meaning from the author to the translator, and then, hopefully, to the reader. It is always a gift. As with the poems in the other two sections, there are contexts and references that are not shared, except in the absolute sense of the gift. Once it is given to you, it's also no longer mine. I recently came upon this statement, near the beginning of Bachelard's *Poétique de l'espace*. It speaks to what I've just said, as long as we keep in mind that "image" should be understood to include thought: "The poet does not confer on me the past life of an image, and nevertheless the image immediately takes root in me."

Citations are printed in italics, usually with the author's name floating in the right margin – a practice I owe to Robin Blaser, although I'm not sure where he got it.

For the more obscure, but generally public, references, there is now the search engine. The obscurantist can no longer hide from your scrutiny.

Poem 1. *working that translation* is a line from Robin Blaser's poem "The Translator: A Tale."

Poem 3. Bach, his cello suites a constant companion.

Poem 5. See Charles Olson's "Against Wisdom as Such" and H.D.'s *Helen in Egypt*.

Poem 6. Brunetto Latini, Dante's *Inferno*, canto XV.

Poem 8. In Hamilton, Ontario, in the old jail, the second-floor passage from the place of imprisonment to the place of execution was called "the bridge of sighs."

Poems 9, 11, and 17. These Rilke translations are drawn from his book *Vergers, suivi d'autres poèmes français.*

Poem 14. See Rilke's poem "La fontaine," Kenneth Anger's film *Eaux d'artifice,* and Maya Deren's film *Ritual in Transfigured Time.*

Poem 19. "Ivry" is a fragment from Artaud's *Cahier d'Ivry* no. 233, which was published by Gallimard in a facsimile edition. The inclusion of this fragment was an immediate result of hearing and seeing "Ivry" by the Soundwalk Collective with Patti Smith.

ACKNOWLEDGMENTS

Part of "Tracery" was published in *Open Text* 2, edited by Roger Farr (North Vancouver: Capilano University Editions, 2009).

An earlier version of "Morning Songs" was published in the first issue of *Some*, edited by Rob Manery (Vancouver, 2019).

The first poem in the "Morning Songs" section has been translated by François Houle into musical terms and recorded as "Morning Song 1" on the CD *Recoder* (Songlines, 2020).

"Translation" was commissioned for the *Capilano Review* 50th Anniversary Issue, edited by Matea Kulić.

Part of "Délires" was published in *Open Text* 2, edited by Roger Farr (North Vancouver: Capilano University Editions, 2009). The remainder appeared in Adam Katz's *Partial Zine* 3 (2020).

I am grateful to those named above for their hospitality, and to the book's editor, Catriona Strang, for her care and attention to the text, as well as to everyone at Talon who had a hand in making this such a presentable object, and to all those who read or heard these poems at various stages and encouraged me in my folly – a list could never be exhaustive.

EDWARD (TED) BYRNE

was born in Hamilton, Ontario, and moved to Vancouver in the late 1960s. He worked at the Trade Union Research Bureau for many years. He was a member of the KSW collective and board for over fifteen years. Since 2010 he has been a member of the Lacan Salon and currently sits on the board. A poet and translator, he frequently writes on poetry and poetics. He has translated poetry from French, Old French, German, and Italian. Recent books include *Duets* (2018) and *A Flea the Size of Paris: The Old French* fatrasies *&* fatras, with Donato Mancini (2020). With Hilda Fernandez he recently co-edited a collection of theoretical and critical psychoanalytic responses to the pandemic, "In a Time of Plagues" (*Contours Journal* 10 [Fall 2020], SFU Institute for the Humanities). He is currently working on *The Seventh Chamber*, a sequel to his book *Beautiful Lies*, as well as papers on the early Renaissance poet Guido Cavalcanti, the philosopher Anne Dufourmantelle, and the poet Norma Cole.